# What's in this book

This book belongs to

_____

# 我们去购物 Going shopping

## 学习内容 Contents

### 沟通 Communication

说说购物经历
Talk about shopping experiences

说说衣物
Talk about clothes

### 生词 New words

| | |
|---|---|
| ★ 衣服 | clothes |
| ★ 裤子 | trousers |
| ★ 跑步 | to run |
| ★ 买 | to buy |
| ★ 忙 | busy |
| ★ 累 | tired |
| ★ 为什么 | why |
| 爱 | to like |
| 卖 | to sell |
| 运动服 | sportswear |
| 电影 | film |

# Get ready

**1** What TV programme is Hao Hao's family watching?

**2** What is your favourite sport?

**3** How do you and your family spend the weekends?

pǎo bù
跑步

yī fu
衣服

姐姐爱跑步，我爱打篮球。夏天来了，我们没有新衣服。

星期六，爸爸妈妈都不忙，我们一起去买运动服。

"这条裤子真可爱！" 姐姐说。
"我们问问怎么卖。" 妈妈说。

"这两件球衣怎么样？红色好看还是
蓝色好看？"我问大家。

"买衣服比做运动累。为什么？"姐姐问。

"因为你走了很多路。休息一下，我
们去看电影吧。"爸爸说。

# Let's think

**1** Recall the story and circle the correct letters.

1 玲玲喜欢做什么？

a                    b                    c

2 星期六，浩浩、玲玲和爸爸妈妈去了哪里？

a                    b                    c

**2** What items do you and your parents usually buy together? Tick and say.

# New words

1 Learn the new words.

衣服　裤子　买　卖　运动服

电影　为什么？　忙　累　我爱跑步。

There are two suns. Why?

2 Look at your teacher. Which word is he/she acting out? Have a guess and say it in Chinese.

03 **1** Listen and circle the correct pictures.

04 **2** Look at the pictures. Listen to the story a

1 星期日，大家一起做什么？

真累！
为什么？

2 爸爸妈妈的运动服是什么颜色的？

3 谁很累？

我没有运动服。
为什么？
因为我太忙了，没去买。

 因为我跑步了。

你的运动服呢?

你忙什么?

跑步、打篮球……我爱打
篮球!

**Look at the pictures and
discuss with your friend.**

1

💬 他为什么不去玩?

💬 因为他……

2

💬 它很高兴。……

💬 因为它爱……

3

💬 他们也很高兴。……

💬 ……

# Task

What do you do on weekends? Draw a picture or paste a photo below and talk to your friend.

# Game

Find a way out of the maze and answer the cat's questions.

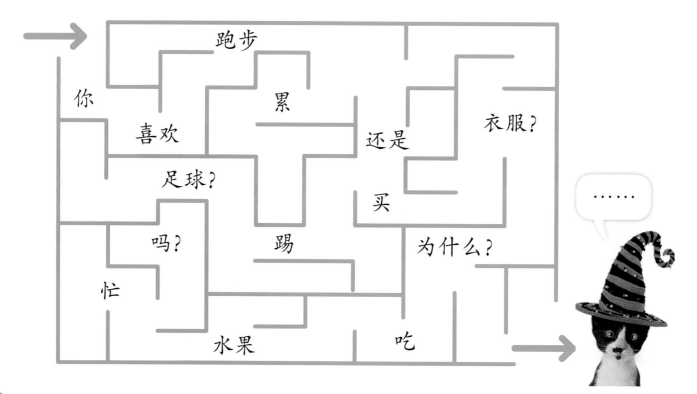

# Chant

Listen and say.

买衣服、买衣服，

爸爸买长裤，妈妈买上衣，

姐姐买短裤，弟弟买球衣。

买衣服、买衣服，

红裤子好看还是蓝裤子好看？

白球衣好看还是黄球衣好看？

买衣服、买衣服，

红色、蓝色、白色、黄色，

长裤、短裤、上衣、球衣都好看。

生活用语 Daily expressions

忙吗？
Are you busy?

听你的！
Up to you!

**1** Trace and write the characters.

、 二 ナ 衣 衣 衣

丿 冂 月 月 服 服 服 服

衣
服

| 衣 | 服 | 衣 | 服 |
|---|---|---|---|
| 衣 | 服 | 衣 | 服 |
| | | | |

**2** Write and say.

这是我的新_____。

我的_____太___了。

**3** Fill in the blanks with the correct words. Colour the correct presents using the same colours.

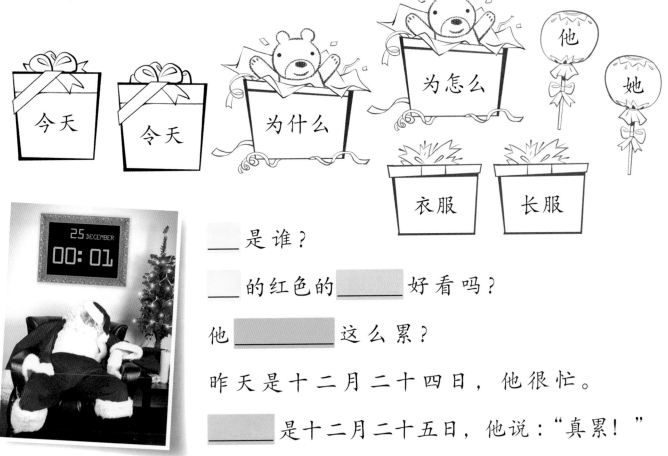

_____ 是谁？

_____ 的红色的 _____ 好看吗？

他 _____ 这么累？

昨天是十二月二十四日，他很忙。

_____ 是十二月二十五日，他说："真累！"

---

## 拼音输入法 Pinyin input

1 Look at the keyboard. Type the 23 consonants listed on the right.

We use the 26 letters on the keyboard to input Pinyin. In the Pinyin system, there are 23 consonants:

| | |
|---|---|
| b p m f | zh ch sh r |
| d t n l | z c s |
| g k h | y w |
| j q x | |

2 Now, type the consonants without looking at the list.

## Cultures

Look at the advertisements for some famous shopping spots around the world. Talk about them with your friend.

Jewellery, carpets, spices ... You name it.

the Grand Bazaar in Istanbul, Turkey

the Damnoen Saduak floating market in Ratchaburi, Thailand

Get a taste of Thailand on boats!

Old paintings, CDs, toys ... Good bargains!

the flea market at the Place du Jeu de Balle in Brussels, Belgium

YOUR DESTINATION FOR SHOPPING

Oxford Street in London, UK

我喜欢……

为什么?

因为……

1. How many of your friends like buying things in shops? How many prefer shopping online? Do a survey and write the numbers.

我喜欢和爸爸妈妈一起去买衣服。

我们喜欢在网上买玩具。

2. Design the home page for a mobile phone shopping application and talk about it with your friend.

**My Design**

浩浩的糖果

玩具
文具
书
衣服
花

玲玲的天地

我喜欢在这里买文具。

这里的糖果很好吃。

你喜欢它吗？为什么？

我……，因为……

**1** Complete the tasks. How many vouchers can you get?

$20 · 买 卖 Read aloud. | BUY BUY | SELL SELL SELL

$30

$30 · 星期六，我和弟弟去跑步。

$30 · 这是 Answ

$50 · 9 a.m. | 3 p.m. CINEMA

$50 · Ask your friend 'Do you like dogs? Why?' in Chinese.

$80

$50 · 你爱做什么？ Look at the pictures and answer in Chinese.

$100 · Make your parents a cup of tea and say 'Are you tired? Please drink some tea.' in Chinese.

妈妈比爸爸忙。

？

inese.

我上午打……，
……

Write the characters.

## 2 Work with your friend. Colour the stars and the chillies.

| Words and sentences | 说 | 读 | 写 |
|---|---|---|---|
| 衣服 | ☆ | ☆ | ☆ |
| 裤子 | ☆ | ☆ | 🌶 |
| 跑步 | ☆ | ☆ | 🌶 |
| 买 | ☆ | ☆ | 🌶 |
| 忙 | ☆ | ☆ | 🌶 |
| 累 | ☆ | ☆ | 🌶 |
| 爱 | ☆ | 🌶 | 🌶 |
| 卖 | ☆ | 🌶 | 🌶 |
| 运动服 | ☆ | 🌶 | 🌶 |
| 电影 | ☆ | 🌶 | 🌶 |
| 为什么？ | ☆ | ☆ | 🌶 |

| | |
|---|---|
| Talk about shopping experiences | ☆ |
| Talk about clothes | ☆ |

## 3 What does your teacher say?

# 分享 Sharing

## Words I remember

| | | |
|---|---|---|
| 衣服 | yī fu | clothes |
| 裤子 | kù zi | trousers |
| 跑步 | pǎo bù | to run |
| 买 | mǎi | to buy |
| 忙 | máng | busy |
| 累 | lèi | tired |
| 为什么 | wèi shén me | why |
| 爱 | ài | to like |
| 卖 | mài | to sell |
| 运动服 | yùn dòng fú | sportswear |
| 电影 | diàn yǐng | film |